Autumn Harvest – Simply Country

by Judy Condon

Library of Congress Cataloging-in-Publications Data
Autumn Harvest – Simply Country by Judy Condon
ISBN 978-0-9847028-3-1

Oceanic Graphic Printing, Inc.
105 Main Street
Hackensack, NJ 07601

Printed in China

Layout and Design by Pat Lucas
Edited by Trent Michaels

Table of Contents

About the Author

Judy Condon is a native New Englander, which is evident in her decorating style and the type of antiques she collects and sells. Her real passion is 19thC authentic dry red or blue painted pieces. While Judy enjoyed a professional career as a teacher, Principal, and Superintendent of Schools in Connecticut, Judy's weekends were spent at her antique shop, *Marsh Homestead Country Antiques*, located in Litchfield, Connecticut.

When her husband, Jeff, was relocated to Virginia, Judy accepted an early retirement from education and concentrated her energy and passion for antiques into a fulltime business. Judy maintains a website, *www.marshhomesteadantiques. com* and has been a Power Seller on eBay® for 13 years under the name "superct".

Judy and her husband Jeff recently returned to their roots in New England and have completed renovating a 19thC cape in Massachusetts. The house was featured in her early 2012 book *Back Home – Simply Country* which included many before and after pictures. Judy has five children and five grandchildren and enjoys reading, golf, bridge, tennis, and volunteering in the educational system in St. Maarten. Judy does her best to provide teaching materials and children's books to the schools in St. Maarten with the hope of helping establish classroomlibraries.

Judy's first 21 books in the "simply country" series, *Country on a Shoestring, Of Hearth and Home – Simply Country, A Simpler Time, Country Decorating for All Seasons, As Time Goes By, Country at Heart, Welcome Home – Simply Country, Home Again – Simply Country, The Warmth of Home, The Country Home, Simple Greens – Simply Country, The Country Life, Simply Country Gardens, Simply Country Gardens, The Spirit of Country, The Joy of Country, Holidays at a Country Home, A Touch of Country, Back Home – Simply Country, Just Country Gardens,* and *The Place We Call Home* have been instant hits and some are in their second printing. Judy continues to pursue additional homes and gardens and is working on five books for publication in 2013. Her books are available on her Website at *www.marshhomesteadantiques.com*, from *Amazon.com*, through her email *marshhomestead@comcast.net*, or by phone at 877-381-6682.

Introduction

It's autumn here in New England. There is a crispness to the air; the trees are treating us to an array of brilliant red and orange colored leaves as a last hurrah before they drop to the ground. It seems everywhere front steps are decorated with bursting large pots of mums in striking rusts, golds and burgundy tones. Purple asters and sedum mix with fading Echinacea and prolong the color in our gardens

Each year as a school teacher, I read a delightful story to my class called Mousekin's Golden House. It told of a little mouse scurrying as winter approached to find a place to spend the winter and while scampering through the meadow; it came upon a discarded jack-o-lantern. Mousekin gathered drieds from the meadow and using the jack-o-lantern's cutout mouth, climbed in and out building a nest. As fall passed, the pumpkin slowly began to decay and, in doing so, the openings of the jack-o-lantern's face began to close as the pumpkin shriveled up. The last picture shows Mousekin nestled inside and the walls of the pumpkin providing a golden glow as the winter winds blew and the snow fell outside.

Much like Mousekin, in New England we have started to "button up and hunker down" as my grandfather used to say. The screens in the windows have been replaced with the storms, the summer clothes in the closets and bureaus have been changed out with the heavier ones stored in the attic or under the bed, and the aroma in the house has changed to that of apple pie and the traditional Yankee pot roast with carrots, onions and potatoes. The patio furniture is put away, the garden beds put to rest and the firewood cut and stacked. We are ready to "hunker down", curl up by the fire and be rejuvenated over the darker days of winter.

As I look around the house, it occurs to me that I have decorated with the harvests of others. My dough bowls are filled with dried Indian corn, my buckets overflow with corn husk tops, dried Sweet Annie, and gooseneck gourds adorn my front door and chimney cupboard in the Keeping Room and freshly cut bittersweet from the meadow tucked everywhere space will allow. The colors of my harvested produce are drab for the most part, but soothing. In *Autumn Harvest – Simply Country*, you will tour the homes of nine families; some of whom have also gathered their autumn harvests to decorate their homes. You will visit two homes in Massachusetts, one home in Connecticut, three homes in Ohio and three homes in Kentucky.

Traditionally, autumn is a time of reflection and a time to give thanks for all our blessings. I'm mindful of that and thankful for my many blessings – not the least of which is you, my readers and friends.

Chapter 1

Betty and Peter Davidian

Betty and Peter Davidian bought their home in East Dennis, Massachusetts in 1999 with the intent to use it as a summer home until their retirement. Ten years later, they sold their home in Holden, MA and moved to the Cape as their year round residence. Their home is a half-cape built by Deacon Daniel Hall. The oldest part dates to 1723. Betty and Peter added the mudroom addition to the side of the house which opens into a large Great Room with cathedral ceiling. Betty and Peter have been the proprietors of davidian-americana for over forty years and specialize in early American country pieces with original paint and surface. Although retired, they continue to participate in shows and are members of the Cape Cod Antique Dealers Association. Peter and Betty sell by appointment only but do maintain a booth and case at the Sandwich Antique Center on Rt. 6A in Sandwich, Massachusetts. The exterior of their home was featured in the garden book, *Just Country Gardens*.

The Living room is painted with Olde Century "Olde Ivory" paint. The lovely wainscoting is original to the house. Two pieces of blue spongeware, most likely with Pennsylvania origin, are displayed on the mantel. The framed picture is a silk work rendering of a religious event, perhaps Rebekkah at the Well. It dates to circa 1825. The portrait to the right of the mantel is one of a pair found in an early home in Holden. They were in disrepair when Betty and Peter bought them for resale but after restoration, which took six years, they decided to keep them.

Hanging over the mantel in the original oval frame, a sailor's farewell is unique in that it is depicted with children. A small ship can be seen in the distance.

The other portrait in the pair is seen hanging over the flame stitch couch from the Angel House in Brookfield, Massachusetts. A mahogany Chippendale arm chair with John D. Rockefeller provenance stands beside a secretary with Boston origin. Betty and Peter purchased it in the 1980's from a Cape Cod dealer. Peter and Betty looked for a long time to find a butler's tray with a more suitable lower side for use as a coffee table.

The wing chair is an older chair which has been reupholstered. The shelf between the windows was chosen because of the wonderful cut shape of the sides.

Peter and Betty sold many of their early soft paste and Staffordshire pieces when they moved but saved some of their favorite pieces which they've displayed on the shelf.

A Hepplewhite Spider Leg candlestand with turned base is tucked in the corner. It holds a brass candlestick and snuffer, a potted flower and an antique book on botany. A miniature oil painting of a house leans on the ledge in back.

A child's wheelbarrow with original red paint and stenciled horse weathervane on the side holds a collection of fabric print cats which were patented around 1900.

Betty and Peter painted the Keeping Room with Olde Century "Barn Red" paint. The table in the center of the room is a drop leaf, three board top; the mustard over red painted Windsors are reproduction pieces made by Bill Wolstenholme of Warren, Rhode Island.

The fireplace in the Keeping Room is one of two original to the house and shares a chimney with that in the living room. Early pewter chargers fit perfectly on the very narrow mantel and are displayed with a collection of shorebirds, some of which were carved by Peter Peltz, a Sandwich, Massachusetts bird carver.

A child's chair with splint seat sits on the hearth and holds a contemporary Raggedy Ann doll.

Peter and Betty couldn't resist the early fire bucket initialed with the letter "D". The 19thC stepback cupboard in original oxblood red paint holds some of Betty's Nicholas Mosse pottery collection.

Betty collects tomato pin cushions which were popular in the 1930's and 40's and are still relatively easy to find. A portion of her collection is seen in the tin-lidded apothecary jars on top. There are also a few strawberry cushions displayed as well. A very rare Roosevelt Bear Pitcher by the Buffalo Pottery Co. sits behind in the center.

A large carved Canada goose is displayed on the 19thC 6' long work table with drawer and scrub top. Peter found the table in a basement spattered with paint; now restored, Betty uses it as a serving table.

A black early ladderback chair holds an early Raggedy Andy doll and blue and white homespun. A vintage blue and white checked bonnet is draped on the back.

The small ladies wing chair is early. Beside it, a 19thC jelly cupboard with original red paint holds a York pottery lamp, lidded box and pewter teapot.

The top painting on the wall is an oil on board of Scargo Hill, the neighborhood where the Davidian's live.

I think the circa 1840 two tiered candle box in dry red paint has wonderful lines. It holds candles, drieds and a clay pipe.

Tucked in a corner of the mudroom which connects the Keeping room and the Great Room, a green pie safe, with original tins, holds a collection of early Steiff bears.

The miniature wheelbarrow in mustard paint was purchased in New York at the Fall Folk Art Show and was chosen because it is initialed PD; in reality for Police Department not Peter Davidian! It is a replica of the wheelbarrows which would have followed and cleaned up after the horses in a parade. The floral hooked rug dates to circa 1930.

Peter and Betty started the Great Room addition in December 2007 and completed it in June 2008. Old boards were used for the plank flooring and some of the beams are old as well. A vintage red and white basket quilt is draped over the loft railing. Beneath it and the sign "New Home", an early hooked rug of a rabbit with a red star in each corner is displayed. Betty chose to decorate the room with barnyard animal prints and pieces wherever possible.

The stretcher base 19thC table behind the couch holds a basket of rag balls and two carriers, one of which sits on a blue painted bench.

The lovely blue painted carrier is filled with tallow candles.

The door is an early salvaged piece. The built-in book shelves were designed intentionally to house a large collection of primarily reference books on antiques.

The clock on the mantel is an early pillar and scroll clock by Chauncey Ives. On either side, there is a Staffordshire rooster and a print above each one of rooster cock fights. Symmetrically, over each window a cheese strainer is framed between the beams.

The old apple ladder holds a red and white quilt beside the blue gray stepback cupboard. The cupboard, which dates to the early 19thC, holds a large mix of early mocha and some Don Carpentier pieces. It also holds some pieces of Staffordshire sheep.

Jerome Howes of Vermont, the son of a well known Cape Cod dealer, painted the painting titled, City of Worcester, which hangs behind the crocks and early lanterns.

In keeping with a barnyard theme in the room, an oil on canvas portrait of sheep hangs beneath a grouping of stick legged wooly sheep on the beam above. Notice the interesting lampshade made with an early coverlet. It was created by Susan Hoyt of Meeting House Antiques at the Black Angus Antiques Mall in Adamstown, Pennsylvania. A stack of graduated sized firkins stands beside the doorway leading to the loft.

The portrait over the demi-lune table in white paint, was sold to a customer, restored and then bought back by the Davidians.

The laundry room is behind the mudroom addition. Peter and Betty found the soapstone sink at a salvage yard in New Bedford and had a contractor build the cupboard to support it. A chalk ware carnival cat sits beneath the single drawer pine work table.

Betty uses lidded unglazed clay pots for her canisters on the counter. Early cutting boards cover the white Formica. The trim and hanging shelf are painted with Old Century "Candleberry Green" paint.

The hooked rug above the built-in bench in the eating area was chosen because the colors were a perfect match for the room.

The master bedroom upstairs is found in the old section of the house. The trim is painted with Old Village "Cobblestone" paint. Betty and Peter added the pocket door to create closet space in the room. Vintage quilts, which blend with the color on the painted floor, are displayed at the foot of the 19thC tiger maple pineapple beds.

A collection of ship dioramas is displayed over the mantel. The theme is in keeping with the Cape Cod area. The largest diorama has been created with wooden sails.

A bedroom in the Great Room addition is outfitted with a contemporary bedroom set. The ladderback chair however dates to the 18thC and is a family heirloom of Betty's.

A lovely pastoral oil on canvas painting hangs above the bed.

Davidian-americana is located at 311 Scargo Hill Road, South Dennis, MA 02660 but is open only by appointment. Please call Peter and Betty at 508-385-1341.

Chapter 2

Wanda and Lowell Burton

Wanda and Lowell Burton built their Olive Hill, Kentucky home in 1982 not far from where they grew up. In fact, they were high school sweethearts.

They both have enjoyed collecting and Lowell particularly enjoys going on the trips and looking at antique tractors which frees up Wanda to hunt for antiques for her home and shop. Wanda owns a shop in nearby Grayson, Kentucky, called *Homespun Sisters*. Her sister Janie and she sell country accessories, as well as reproduction and antique larger pieces.

As a shop owner, Wanda has had the good fortune of being able to also decorate her home with pieces she purchases on her business buying trips or those that she occasionally brings home from the shop.

Wanda always liked country pieces but has abandoned what she calls the "cutesy country" for a more primitive look. Whether she's buying for the shop or herself, she admits it is the "thrill of the hunt" that keeps her coming back for more.

Lowell, who is a self-employed contractor, put down the pine floor with new pine planks. Wanda painted the trim with Eddie Bauer "Bittersweet" paint which is a soft gray green color. She purchased the paint at Lowes. Wanda's wing chairs are Johnston Benchworks which she sells in her shop. The red cupboard on the left is a family heirloom which has been rebuilt and refinished to hold the television. The drop leaf table was purchased at a local shop and holds a bail handled pantry box in attic surface. I love the mellow tones of this room.

A sweet little cupboard shown below right, made of poplar, holds candle molds on top. The door is draped with a vintage mustard and green coverlet remnant and early powder horn.

Lowell made the blanket crane which holds a Family Heirloom Coverlet and old basket.

The little lift top desk is one of Wanda's favorite pieces as is the tall clock in the corner which Wanda's brother-in-law, Tony Little, made. She sells his clocks in her shop and had sold this one when the customer came in and said she was selling it. Wanda immediately bought it back and brought it home.

The gameboards and wall box were made by a local folk artist, Pat Rayburn.

Lowell made the mantel and also assembled the gun hanging above it from a kit. Early pantry boxes, old and new pewter and a lantern can be seen on the mantel. The skewers were purchased at Kentucky Roots *owned by Jerrie Cossett. An early oven peel, purchased on a buying trip with Janie, rests on the right side of the mantel.*

Wanda carried the paint trim color into the dining area and also the soothing tones of natural wood and patina. A garland of small gourds is strung across the bowl rack where a garland of dried green beans hangs from the side.

Wanda loves old cutting boards and has a difficult time passing one by.

The black cupboard, which Wanda uses as a side board, was one of the first pieces Wanda bought.

The mustard bucket bench with dry paint was purchased at Spice Ridge, a nearby shop.
The peg rack holds bonnets and aprons made with vintage fabric.
Indian corn and concrete spice rubbed pumpkins, purchased at Olde Glory in Waynesville, Ohio,
fill the trencher also found in Waynesville.

Lowell made the kitchen island with wood from his grandmother's house.

Wanda found the early dough box in mustard paint at the nearby Creek Cabin Antique Shop.

Wanda's counters are Corian. The back splash is tile which Lowell installed. Wanda uses the little black apothecary to hold her paperwork.

The furniture in the living room is also Johnston Benchworks. Wanda has decorated this room in black and white check. The standing doughbox, which she uses as a coffee table, was found in West Virginia. The table under the window was made by Lowell using old wood he had salvaged. The mustard chair in the corner was a Christmas gift from Wanda's sons. Wanda's window treatments are Family Heirloom Weaver linen.

A friend found the spinning wheel for Wanda in Sandy Hook, Kentucky.

The whale tail wall shelf is a new piece. It holds pewter and redware pieces from Turtle Creek Potters.

The black bentwood chair is a contemporary piece. The shelf above, a reproduction, holds more redware and pewter. The large cupboard with original dry blue paint holds pantry boxes and stoneware crocks which Lowell likes to collect.

A red stepback, shown above, holds more of the same and a lovely early carrier with great patina.

The bed in the master bedroom is covered with a Family Heirloom Weaver coverlet. An early coverlet remnant hangs over the blanket crane in the corner.

The black bonnet on top of the dresser was Lowell's grandmother's Sunday bonnet. The portrait above it is a reproduction. An early lidded box with original red paint stands on top of the dresser.

In the guestroom, a shelf holds fabric covered pantry boxes and bonnets made by local artisan, Margaret Garven.

The large stepback in the corner is a reproduction. As Wanda so aptly put it, "It doesn't matter if you mix old and new. It's the look we want to achieve."

The apothecary, a new piece, stands beside an old lantern on top of the chest of drawers.

Margaret Garven made the bonnet, seen below, and the little seed sack, seen left from an old coverlet scrap.

Homespun Sisters, *located at 18 S Carol Malone Road in Grayson, Kentucky is open Monday-Saturday, 10-5. Their website is www.homespunsisters.com. They may be reached by phone at 606-474-5296 or email homespunsisters@yahoo.com*

Chapter 3

Anita and Daniel McCann

Anita and Daniel McCann have lived in the Seaman, Ohio home they built for the last twenty years and are ready to move on. Just as we country decorators change our homes around on a daily basis it seems, Anita has completely changed what she collects and how she decorates. She wants to sell their Victorian home and build a smaller saltbox on two of the four acres they own. Over the years, Anita admits she has continued to be more primitive in her collecting and décor and Daniel has jumped right in by utilizing his talents as a craftsman to help her make it happen. Anita gets many of her ideas from books and refers to the "simply country book" series to show Daniel just what she has in mind and would like him to build.

Anita has an eye for a great bargain and seems to know where to shop. For example, the table with red wash base, which she uses as their coffee table in the living room, was one she found at a barn sale for $35. On it she has placed some treen; a plate, cup and two wooden bowls. The blue cupboard hanging on the wall, which holds bowls and measures, was in total disrepair when Anita found it. She knew Daniel could rebuild it which he did . Daniel was able to create a milk paint and finish the piece to look brand "new-old".

Anita used a paint on her walls similar in color to oatmeal. She has begun the process of painting the trim and is slowing making her way throughout the house feeling that it gives the rooms a more country look. Anita found the corner cupboard with attic surface for $100 and believes it was the top half of a larger piece. It holds many pieces of old and new pewter. As Anita finds an old piece, she changes out a new piece.

The child's cradle in dry red is draped with a vintage textile. A black folk art doll peeks over the top.

Anita found the 18thC mantel which Daniel enhanced with wide boards when they converted the fireplace to a gas insert. Daniel then painted the entire piece a country red with a black overpaint to age it. An early cutting board provides a back drop for a large pewter plate. The blanket crane above holds an egg basket.

Anita at one time provided child care to several children. One of the children's father worked on a farm and Anita asked him to look out for a pie safe for her. It didn't take long before he came back and said he had found one. He bought it from the farmer for $5 and sold it to Anita for $25; everyone seemed to be happy with the deal each made! It retains its original surface and holds a six board pine chest and large egg basket.

Daniel made the corner cupboard from old boards and painted the inside a powder blue; his favorite color. Anita took no time to fill the shelves with a variety of early treen bowls.

Anita has placed an apple stirrer over the peg rack which holds a lantern, a large bowl, scoop and bonnets made by Anita's sister- in- law.

Daniel built an addition on the side of the house which he designed as an octagonal shape to maximize the light and windows. Anita tea-dyed bed sheets to create the window treatments.

Daniel made the make-do chair from an old ladderback chair they found. The large single door cupboard in the corner was bought for $395 from a country antique dealer who was closing his store and didn't want to have to move it.

The slant top wall desk in black paint is old. Above it hangs a reproduction portrait. The stool was purchased at the Springfield Ohio Antique Show.

Anita and Daniel's dining area is at one end of the kitchen. Daniel made the chimney cupboard using an old door and then matched the paint on the sides. The light over the table was a great find! Anita paid $5 for it and is taking it with her to their new home.

The farm table was a Valentine's Day present to Anita from Daniel. It was found in Kentucky and cost $50 but required a great deal of restoration which Daniel was able to do with the help of Anita's cousin. Daniel made the hornbeam on the center of the table.

Daniel also made the sawbuck table and the hanging apothecary with old boards. A friend gave Anita the boards with blue paint and Daniel was able to create the rest of the piece incorporating the boards and then matching the paint to blend it all together.

Twenty years ago, Daniel and Anita originally planned to build a log home and purchased the logs with that intent. After years of having the logs sitting in a pile, Daniel split them and faced the walls of a spare room to create a 'log cabin' addition. The buttery has special meaning to Anita as Daniel made it from wood from her father's barn.

Shelves are lined with measures, firkins, pails, another hornbeam Daniel made, as well as, a carrier filled with cookie molds. Daniel also made the standing candle stick.

The hanging bowl rack is a reproduction which Anita was drawn to because of the cutout sides.

More bonnets, made by Anita's sister-in-law, are displayed on a peg rack beside a broom made by Daniel from "corn broom"; a bunch of which is seen in the barrel on the floor.

A huge gourd can be seen in the trencher on the table Daniel reproduced from one Anita saw in an earlier "simply country" book.

The dry sink in the back is a reproduction piece which Daniel painted with his blue milk paint mixture.

A basket on the floor holds flax and an early hatchel.

The cupboard over the couch was found at a local shop and is early. The dry sink on the right is also early and Daniel created the cupboard above it then painted it to match. I think he has a real talent to match paint colors.

Daniel built Anita another mantel in the kitchen to give her more display space. The little apothecary in blue paint is one of Daniels' creations. Behind the sink, a wonderful small spice box with lovely patina holds a miniature basket.

A variety of gourds fills the bowl on the table.

Another small hornbeam, made by Daniel, holds a collection of early spoons.

Anita used the recipe from Simple Greens to create the Bundt cake on the early table which serves as an island. The bowl beside it is filled with nuts and apple cinnamon sticks.

Chapter 4

Alyce and Larry North

A country auction was responsible for bringing Alyce and Larry together! Larry North was born and raised in Gallipolis, Ohio and was in the process of building a log home when tragically his wife passed away. Alyce Mulkey, who grew up in Kenova, West Virginia but spent most of her adult life in nearby eastern Kentucky, lost her husband around the same time. Larry and Alyce attended a country auction and were both perusing a collection of Civil War pictures when Larry, who recognized Alyce from an antique show, introduced himself. For the past eight years they have been enjoying their blended family of five children and four grandchildren AND decorating their log home with country antiques.

Alyce is retired from the Department of Veteran Affairs where she worked for 31 years and has just recently opened an antique shop in an outbuilding on their property. Larry is a retired Physical Education teacher and particularly enjoys collecting stoneware pieces that were produced locally.

The two rocking chairs, seen on the expansive front porch, were purchased the night Larry and Alyce met at the auction. An early buggy seat in green paint sits beneath the double window. The ceramic figure, fondly referred to as Charlie, belonged to Larry's mother and sat on her front steps for over fifty years.

Alyce purchases gourds at a local flea market from a man who grows them locally and makes musical instruments with them. She has filled an early goat cart and a large grain bin. Sweet Annie fills the painted box on the wall behind it and provides a "marsh-like" backdrop for a mallard decoy.

When you enter the North's home, you step into a large room filled with primitives and a "his" and "her" couch! The huge bowl on the 8' long early chest holds some of Alyce's vintage stone fruit.

The blue-gray painted cupboard with yellow doors creates a divided wall and backs up to another cupboard behind it in the kitchen area. This cupboard is filled with some of Larry's stoneware from Gallipolis, Ohio and Palestine, West Virginia. Alyce likes to collect coverlets; some of which are seen displayed on the top shelf and also the bottom cubby of the cupboard. Alyce also loves to collect early painted boxes and chests. The chest on the top right in dry blue paint is an early merchant's egg box stamped Gallipolis, Ohio on the side.

Next to the stairway is a jeweler's cupboard in blue gray paint which Alyce was drawn to because it reminded her of her father's cabinets he used as a clockmaker. A small stool stacked on top holds another one of Alyce's painted crates. Tucked beneath the bench, an architectural iron star rests against the back.

Alyce loves to collect gameboards. She started with many reproduction pieces then changes them out when she finds an authentic early painted board.

A spectacular lidded doughbox holds a collection of vintage spools at the center of an apple green painted farm table in the dining area. Hanging on the wall to the left of the window, a hunt board holds a collection of vintage peanut butter tins in a variety of colors. The large piece in front of the window is an Amish churn.

A corner cupboard with glass doors retains its original apple green paint. Beside the cupboard, an early calendar clock was repaired by Alyce's Dad. Alyce has been trying to talk Larry into removing the paint from the top of the table and she says it is the ONLY piece they have not yet been able to compromise on.

Larry and Alyce use an old store front counter to house their kitchen sink. Another example of Alyce's passion is seen on the counter to the right – early spice boxes. The cutting board behind the chalkboard has remnants of the alphabet and was from a local school.

The mustard pie safe, seen below left, came out of an early country store in nearby Gallia County. Alyce has filled the shelves with a collection of butter presses which she started to collect after receiving one belonging to her grandmother. An early grain carrier holds a collection of treen bowls on top and beside it, an early treen double measure. A middle shelf holds a trencher filled with vintage rag balls.

A unique stepback in dry red paint with green paneled doors serves as the pantry. Bringing it home on the back of the truck, Alyce and Larry lost the top half of the cupboard on a steep hill which they now refer to as "Step Back Hill". A local Amish craftsman repaired the damage and it's as good as "old".

Larry drove to Iowa to purchase the vintage stove replica. Alyce has lamented more than once that having been accustomed to cooking for a large family in the past, this oven won't hold anything larger than an 11 lb. turkey which makes family gatherings a challenge. Alyce says she has become accustomed to doing a lot of rotisserie and ordering out! (I didn' think that sounded so bad!)

The blue stepback seen left backs up to the large cupboard in the front room and helps to divide the room. It holds pots and pans while on top a collection of blue and white stoneware water coolers can be seen. The grain bin has a lid that slides back similar to a server's cabinet.

Alyce and Larry's favorite piece is the standing apothecary with dry red paint. It was in total disrepair when they found it and a friend, who happened to be an expert carpenter, restored the piece. Stacks of pantry boxes are displayed on top.

Alyce and Larry use an old store counter, found in Nebraska, as an island. One side has the red paint with drum drawers which roll back, while the other side is flat with cream colored early paint. Large gourds, found locally, fill a carrier at the end of the counter. A 19thC dry sink in red paint provides additional storage space and fits perfectly at the end. The "steak" wooden sign over the stove was the first antique piece Alyce ever purchased.

One of Alyce's coverlets is draped over the four poster bed in the master bedroom. The six-board chest at the foot of the bed retains original red paint and dates to the mid 19thC

Alyce was able to purchase the early cherry corner cupboard from her mother's minister's estate. It is wide enough to provide ample space to display more of Alyce's coverlet collection.

The desk in front of the window is a Civil War era piece. The cupboard beside it in the corner holds a television.

An early china doll, belonging to Alyce as a child, sits in a basket beside a rabbit made for Alyce by her grandmother. The large corner cupboard was purchased with only the front doors and shelves. A local carpenter rebuilt the piece and added crown molding. A barn ladder holds a red and white coverlet next to it.

Alyce found the primitive child's chair at The Catlettsburg Antique Center where she maintains a booth.

In a second guestroom, the desk in the corner with early mustard paint came from a doctor's office and still had receipts and a prescription pad in the drawer. A vintage red and white quilt is draped over the foot of the bed.

Beneath the window, the footed chest in blue green paint is an old divided grain bin which Alyce uses as a hamper. The divided boxes make it ideal for separating light and dark clothes!

The early cream and apple green hanging cupboard is in the master bath. An early decoy sits on top.

Three aprons hang on a rack in the downstairs bathroom.

Notice the wonderful form and patina on the carrier at the edge of the tub which Alyce uses to hold soaps and shampoos.

Note also the early clock which Alyce's Dad made from four old clocks.

What great dry blue paint on the buggy bench tucked next to the commode. A shelf above the commode holds chalky white pieces and of sentimental value is the Big Ben alarm clock belonging to Alyce's father..

Painted early buckets sit on top of a small chest above the blue jelly cupboard which Alyce uses to hold linens.

On the back of the house, a large porch, like the one in front, only screened, is filled with country pieces including a large swing belonging to Larry's grandmother.

An ice cream maker with blue paint looks great against the chalky white paint of the cupboard it rests on. A pump stands on a small drop leaf table in green paint.

Alyce's shop is called North Log Cabin Antiques. It is located at her home in Gallipolis, OH and is open by appointment. To make an appointment, please call 740-379-9093 or email her at alycelynn@msn.com. Alyce also rents space at Catlettsburg Antique Mall in Catlettsburg, KY.

Alyce commented on how the "simply country book" series allows enough pictures of homes that it is easy to recognize the pride and love each person has in their home. It certainly is the case with the North's home!

Chapter 5

Elsie and John Newsom

Elsie and John Newsom were both born in Connecticut and have been collecting for over fifty years, but . . . imagine the good fortune to have inherited antiques from their parents in a style they would have chosen to purchase! John's parents lived next door in an 1810 Colonial to where John and Elsie currently reside. Elsie was brought up in a home that was less formal than John's parents and she attributes her love of a more formal look to her mother-in-law. For the past twenty years, Elsie admits they enjoy collecting earlier pieces.

John and Elsie have lived in their Gambrel roof home for the last 43 years. They built the house in 1968 from plans they found in American Homes Magazine. Both enjoy collecting the same period antiques and John takes an active role in collecting samplers and pewter which they have collected since the days when pewter could be purchased for a little more than pennies.

The portrait over the camelback sofa in the living room is of Jack's grandfather, Dr. Carroll Beach. The Paul Revere lantern was a gift from a neighbor when they moved to Maine.

A pair of fiddle back Queen Anne chairs surrounds an early oval tip-top table. Pewter plates and bowls, some of which are English, are displayed on top.

An early drop leaf butterfly table dating to the late 18thC was a gift from Allan Carr, the former curator of the Stanton House Museum in Clinton. Resting on top is a gameboard and early clay marbles found at a shop in nearby Westbrook.

The six-board chest is a family piece and holds a small stack of pantry boxes, small bench and early tin lantern. The plate rack above it was made by John and Elsie's son-in-law from plans found in *Country Living* magazine.

The decoy was found at a shop in Woodbury, CT and the treen plate behind it purchased from MacKay and Field Antiques.

Elsie has placed a carriage bench seat, found in Camden, Maine, on top of a pine drop leaf table. The burl bowl was purchased from the late John Henry, an antique dealer in Wiscasset, Maine. The bench beneath the table was a gift from Allan Carr. The early Chippendale mirror above was passed to John and Elsie from John's parents.

Elsie and John had to remove the base of the corner cupboard to fit it into their living room. It is filled with some of John's pewter collection. The sampler beside it dates to 1833 and was purchased at an antique show in Stratford, CT.

The family room, painted with Benjamin Moore "Georgian Brick" paint, provides lots of space to display both American and English pewter. Notice the large charger on the floor. It measures almost 26" in diameter and is an English piece.

A child's high chair, belonging to John's family, holds a small cloth doll. Beside the chair, early shoe forms hang from the mantel. A graduated set of measures lines the mantel filling almost the entire space to the whale oil lamp at the right side.

A reproduction heart trivet holds early tin strainers. Elsie and John found the small Victorian sled at the York Antique Show in Pennsylvania.

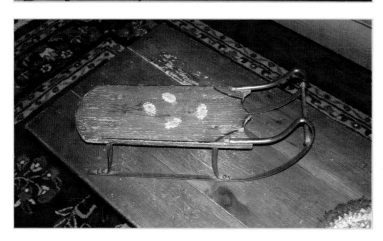

The secretary desk, dating to the 19thC, was inherited from John's family. Elsie hooked the mat on the back of the fireside chair beside it.

The sitter in the portrait over the couch is unidentified.

The bucket bench seen left holds a collection of brown manganese jugs and crocks. Elsie and John found the bench in Wiscasset, Maine.

Elsie and John have placed a set of Windsor chairs on either side of an old sawbuck table they found in Massachusetts. A large burl bowl rests on the center.

A plate rack holds a collection of small wooden bowls and tin collectibles. The rack was found in Maine. The drop leaf table was inherited and stands beside an early slat back chair with mushroom finials. A large redware bowl stands on the table beside a carved shorebird.

Elsie purchased the standing doughbox at a local shop. The color and size were perfect for the room.

The two portraits on board hanging above were inherited from Allan Carr. The small pine apothecary chest was purchased at American Harvest Antiques in Paducah, KY. The candlestick was purchased in England.

Elsie and John removed the glass doors on the corner cupboard, seen above, to give it an earlier look. It is filled with original pieces of redware and slipware found in Connecticut and Pennsylvania.

Elsie made the small tin candlestick on top of the pantry box. The carved bird beside it is not old.

A courting candlestick and wooden house made by folk artist, Christopher Gurshin stand on top of a slant top desk purchased at a shop in Sheffield, Massachusetts.

Elsie and John were disappointed to learn that the red stepback cupboard seen left was sold by the time they arrived at the Wilton Antique Show. The dealer who had sold it suggested they contact the person who had purchased it. Elsie and John did just that, bought it and the dealer was willing to deliver it for them. It is filled with slipware and unglazed redware. A beef platter, purchased in Willington Connecticut, rests behind a treen bowl of stone fruit standing on the bottom shelf.

A candlebox found in Kentucky hangs above a doll chair given to Elsie and John from Allan Carr.

The kitchen table was purchased from Corinne Burke. The Shaker chairs were found in West Townsend, Massachusetts.

A neighbor convinced Elsie to remove the cupboard doors to give the kitchen an earlier look. Elsie painted the cupboards and was initially disappointed that they were too light but over time the color has darkened - just as her neighbor said they would.

Elsie and John purchased the bucket bench at a local shop and the butter churn with blue paint in Wiscasset, Maine.

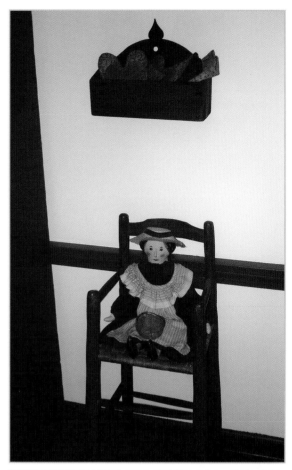

Elsie's counters are made of cherry which she finds very easy to maintain. Assorted treenware is displayed at the back of each counter. The small cutting board over the stove was purchased during a trip to France.

The apothecary on the counter was found in Maine and stands beside a large burl mortar and pestle.

Elsie displays textiles and baskets in a small hanging cupboard in the first floor bathroom. I thought Elsie's idea to hide the tank of the commode was great! An early textile has been fitted over the top.

Sue Dwyer, an artist from Rhode Island, aged the walls in the master bedroom upstairs. Elsie covered the bed with a linen coverlet purchased at Ginny Curry's in Ohio.

The lift-top desk, purchased from the late John Henry in Maine, holds another wooden house crafted by artist Christopher Gurshin. An early sampler hangs on the wall above.

Elsie took a class and made the primitive wooden candlestand beside the bed.

Elsie and Jack inherited the beautiful highboy seen right. It holds a wall paper box on top.

Elsie covered the bed in a second spare room with burlap giving the reproduction bed an early, primitive look. She aged the walls with burnt umber to achieve the same result.

The hooded cradle was found in West Townsend, MA

Early textiles hang on a peg rack in the corner. A stack of fabric covered round boxes stands below.

The small wall shelf in the corner holds a collection of painted tinware .

Elsie and John use the screened porch off the kitchen as much as weather permits.

In addition to overlooking the flower beds in the front, the back overlooks a small shed which Elsie would like to make into a guesthouse some day; perhaps finished on the interior like a log cabin.

Now both retired, Elsie reports that no matter what country they are traveling to, they are always looking for antiques. When home, Elsie enjoys rug hooking and making holiday crafts for friends.

Chapter 6

❧ ✿ ❧

Vina and Ralph Miller

Ralph and Vina Miller, both native Kentuckians, were high school sweethearts and have been married 40 years. In the 1990's, Ralph and Vina Miller bought land in Ashland, Kentucky to stable horses for their grandchildren, never intending to use the property for any other purpose. In 2006, the house on the adjoining property came up for sale, and Ralph and Vina decided to buy it as rental property. Instead, they ended up moving in themselves three years ago and haven't regretted their decision. The house was built in the late 1800's and was originally a one-room schoolhouse named Golden Rod School. The Class of 1936 was the last to graduate. Vina often meets former students who share stories about the school. The porch across the front was added later.

Ralph and Vina essentially gutted the house and hired a carpenter from New England, who used his experience and input from Vina to create the exact home they had in mind. Vina said more than once during our interview that the carpenter took her input and expertly re-created her vision; Vina never saw the finished product until the very end.

Vina loves gourds and displays this large example that she waited a few years to own, as her friend wasn't quite ready to part with it. It sits on the front porch on a sawbuck table Ralph and Vina use in the yard for picnics.

Ralph and Vina found the early piece of farm equipment in the loft of the barn on the property. The dry red paint made it worthy of a spot on the front porch. It is stamped on the side 'Grain Grater – Ohio'.

Vina filled a flea market find basket with drieds from the garden and perched a black crow on top as a final touch to her door decoration.

Vina decorated the door to the buttery with early barrels, carriers, dried sunflowers, and a dry painted white table.

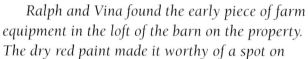

In the parlor, Vina has used a late 19thC carpenter chest as a table in front of the couch. The brown painted wall box is a new piece.

The lowboy seen right is an early piece and retains its original teardrop handles. A large demi-john jug stands on top beside a redware plate from David T. Smith. A primitive cricket stool stands in front of an early arm chair with knuckle arms.

The desk in the corner is one of Vina's favorites, a two-piece secretary with original pulls. The wood is perhaps oak and gives the piece a grain-painted look. Vina and Ralph's carpenter built all the paneled interior window shutters. To save money, Vina chose paint colors from historic samples and then had her carpenter match the colors with paint from Walmart. This trim paint is called "Smokey Mountains".

Vina found the perfect spot inside the desk for an old wallpaper box. A pewter bowl holds stone fruit on a small pine desk; Vina liked its peg construction throughout.

An early pipe box with two clay pipes hangs between the windows. The candlestand beside the chair holds a slide top candlebox and candle nippers. On the floor, an early basket holds a niddy-noddy and rag balls.

The large black paneled cupboard holds a television as well as two early coverlets on top. Vina finds almost all of her pieces locally. Ralph travels a great deal working as an industrial sandblaster and painter; once he is home, he wants to stay home.

A Bellarmine jug rests atop the long farm table, shown below left. Vina purchased the chair from an antique dealer who described it as a Barley Twist English chair. It features a William and Mary style and has a crewel padded seat.

A grouping of three pewter pieces adorns one end of the mantel while a treenware trencher rests at the opposite end. Dried herbs can be seen hanging from the mantel as well as an oil Betty lamp.

Vina bought the cant back shelf beside the fireplace from a dealer friend after it didn't sell at a show. It is pegged construction and has a Spanish brown milk paint surface. Vina has filled the shelves with treen and particularly likes the heart cut in the handle of the carrier on the second shelf. A dipper made from a gourd can be seen hanging on the side.

A large stepback holds shelves of old pewter. Of particular interest is the large early pewter flagon purchased at a flea market for $5.

I love the colors Vina uses in her kitchen. Vina told her carpenter she wanted old hinges and recessed paneled doors and this is what she got. She never saw them until after they were installed and was thrilled with the result. Vina's countertops are black Formica.

Vina uses tobacco panels as window treatments throughout most of the house. The redware plate with tulip pattern in the corner is a David T. Smith piece. Measures and stoneware line the back of the counters while an early bread peel hangs above.

The neutral tones of the large bee skep on top of the cupboard blend beautifully with the tan colors in the room. Even the floor cloth, done in tans and black, tie the room together.

The large bin on the floor reads 'BREAD' across the front. A bread basket with an Ohio star in the center leans on top. The reproduction rack above holds a collection of new redware pieces, most of which are David T. Smith.

A large gray reproduction cupboard stands beside the doorway leading to the buttery. The cupboard is filled with stoneware and treen. A large basket with an unusual wooden hook – the reason Vina bought the basket-rests on top.

The picture left shows the layout of the Keeping Room. The table with chunky legs is a reproduction and seats 10. A blue-gray cupboard in the corner holds an early bucket filled with gourds and an early dough bowl with lovely patina. A breadboard with dried herbs hangs on one side. Above, a candle dryer purchased at nearby Kentucky Roots holds more dried herbs.

Vina found the pine hutch table at the Route 60 yard sale which occurs every August; the yard sale stretches for over 10 miles. A lovely multi-colored woven coverlet is draped across the back. The whale tail shelf above is a reproduction. The fluted pewter platter was a gift to Vina from her son.

Vina believes the room she uses off the kitchen as the buttery may have been a root cellar or cold storage area. The unheated room may have been used to keep potatoes when the house was a working farm. Vina found the hanging scales at Kentucky Roots. The barrel in the dry sink belonged to Vina's late brother. A string of dried gourds hangs beneath a make-do shelf that holds a basket and standing candle mold.

A wool bag marked '1857' and shears hang with herbs and a bonnet from a peg rack in the opposite corner. Vina purchased the bag at Spice Ridge, another nearby shop. On a large barrel, a manganese jug holds a candle. Also displayed are a powder horn, large sugar cone, and cloth sack filled with, as Vina described, plum grannies.

A small wall box filled with bags of tea and a peel hang above an old wooden shovel and small bucket bench.

The drab olive cupboard seen left is Vina's favorite piece. She added a smaller shelf on top to display unglazed redware crocks, sugar cones, Rockingham, and a set of glass jars purchased at Kentucky Roots.

A small gathering basket rests in the cubby of a small box in the bathroom. An apple green bench holds two buckets.

Beside the window, a peg rack displays a collection of early bonnets.

A seed sack hangs from the left side of a small wall cabinet over the commode. Vina uses a piece of linen as a towel alongside.

Vina purchased the cradle seen at the foot of the bed because of its unusual shape and single wide-board construction.

A yarn winder stands in front of the window beside a basket filled with wool.

In the corner, Vina has placed a slant top desk on top of a painted blanket chest.

Vina used the same tan paint on the trim and floors of the room to contrast with the black bed – a similar color combination as the kitchen's.

Chapter 7

Pam and Rick Howard

Pam and Rich Howard had always wanted a wooden house so when the ten year old home in Sandy Hook, Kentucky came on the market with 107 acres, they jumped at the chance to own it. Pam feels this is the closest they could come to owning a log home. When Pam began collecting about twenty-five years ago, she collected Victorian and Flow Blue, Blue Willow and Gray/Blue Spatterware. With the purchase of this home, the wooden floors, ceilings and walls lent themselves to a more primitive décor and Pam has jumped in with both feet. In eight short years, Pam has filled the house with primitives inside and out.

A large covered porch creates additional space for Pam to display barrels and birdhouses. The rockers seem to scream "come sit awhile"!

A pair of gourds hangs on a large slaw cutter at one end of the porch. An early primitive blue table holds some of Pam's early spatterware collection.

Look at the wonderful lines the wood on the walls, ceiling and wood floor create. The living room is at one end of the large space. A large trencher holds a mustard and black coverlet. The pine chest dates to the 19thC and has large hand cut dovetails. Pam found the sofa at a yard sale for $50 and had it reupholstered in the mustard check.

Three piggins are displayed on the hearth while above ,the mantel holds some of Pam's pewter collection.

Pam purchased the pine bowl rack because of the wonderful cut out sides and large dovetails in the back.

Rick and Pam found the pie safe with mustard paint in Morehead Kentucky at The Shaving Horse shop. It is filled with stoneware and pantry boxes. A stack of firkins can be seen on the left. Rick enjoys antiquing as much as Pam and Pam is the first to admit she wouldn't have as many things if Rick didn't always encourage her to buy them; warning her if she hesitates it will be gone when she returns to buy it. Rick particularly likes to collect stoneware; two large pieces fill the top of the safe.

Pam isn't sure if the lovely pine cupboard with the screen front was a pie or cheese safe. She just was drawn to the patina. Rick and Pam found the piece in West Virginia at a shop owned by Mary and Bill Rose.

Pam uses tobacco panels on her windows. A small bucket bench purchased at Kentucky Roots in Louisa, Kentucky holds measures and stoneware crocks. The large #6 brown churn provides a resting spot for a large breadboard; a gift from Pam's sister-in-law.

The picture above shows the expanse of the room with the stairs separating the living room from the dining area. The dome- lidded trunk in front of the sofa is dated 1866 and looks to have been originally painted a blue/green paint. It was found in Maysville, Kentucky and retains its original iron straps

Pam used a trim color called "Jamestown Red" purchased at Tru Value Hardware. A large dough box with original dry red paint holds gourds and bittersweet on the farm table.

Between the windows, a pine dry sink with high apron back holds tin, a large standing candlemold, sap bucket and small wooden scoop. The small cricket stool is holding a fly screen.

Pam has chosen to hang a large wooden tray with cut out handles and use it as a back drop for dried flowers. A graduated set of tin scoops hangs across the bottom.

In the entranceway to the kitchen area, the large stepback seen left holds Pam's yellowware collection. Amidst bowls and pitchers, Pam shows milk pans and covered crocks. I like how she has displayed the yellowware rolling pin on the first shelf.

A blue gray stepback holds a large canted apple tray with blue paint. Beside it, Pam uses an early standing candle dryer to display drieds from her garden. Under the herbs, a tall standing piggin churn with original staves stands next to a barrel.

Pam has filled a large measure with cloth sacks marked flour, coffee and sugar.

Pam has placed a winnowing board on the wall and draped a linen remnant on one corner. A wooden scoop is suspended from the top.

Wonderful large stoneware crocks are displayed on top of the open gray painted cupboard beneath the stairs. Pam uses the shelves for measures and smaller pieces of stoneware. A tin grater with scalloped lines provides an interesting texture to the vignette.

Rick made the hanging board with wood given to him by a friend. I love the color of the paint. The bench below, holding a collection of sap buckets was a gift from Pam's sister-in-law.

Pam used the same country red paint on her kitchen cupboards but put it over black to darken it a bit from the trim in the rest of the room. A blue pie safe holds a collection of quilts and provides a divider island between the kitchen and the dining area. It was purchased from Artie and Jack Smoot in Owingsville, Kentucky.

A lovely painted blue green grain bin fits perfectly alongside the refrigerator. It was purchased at Kentucky Roots and holds a large trencher.

A dough bowl holds a variety of butter presses atop the stove. Another winnowing board to the side holds different sizes of tin-lidded jars and a sugar cone.

Pam has many measures which she places around the house. In the kitchen she uses them as canisters and containers for utensils. Pam's countertops are gray formica which she hopes to replace in the near future. To the left of the sink, a wooden dipper can be seen above the stoneware crock holding pieces of treen.

The large standing butcher block table holds a collection of boxes filled with tin. The chunky four legged smaller butcher block was carved from a single piece of wood. The carrier holds a unique grater for baking potatoes in the fireplace.

The lighting in the bedroom seen left accentuates the diagonal lines of the wood on the walls. An early tan patchwork quilt covers the bed which has wooden rails, spool turned posts and all wood peg construction.

A small splay legged stool stands beneath the table Pam uses as a writing desk at the foot of the bed.

A grain scoop to the right of the bathroom sink is ideal as a towel rack. Hanging on the opposite wall, a charcoal sifter holds a smaller box once used as a cheese mold and constructed with wooden pegs.

I couldn't resist including the picture of the early farm wagon located near the barn. It generated a sense of tranquility.

Chapter 8

⌒ ✺ ⌒

Tammy and Vic Weaver

Tammy and Vic Weaver live in Benton, Ohio not far from where they each grew up. Actually they live in the 1830's house that belonged to Tammy's grandfather in the 1950's. He had remodeled it to the 50's and Vic and Tammy were able to buy it from her family in 2005 They gutted the house "right down to the bones" as Tammy called it and began in earnest to restore the house to the 19thC to the point of exposing the original beams. Vic is a Vice President of a bank and Tammy is the buyer and manager of *Country Gatherings*, part of the *Olde Berlin Village Shoppes* located in nearby Berlin, Ohio. As buyer, she has access to the

latest in country accessories and has been fortunate to be able to decorate her home from pieces purchased at the shop. Tammy says "work isn't work"!

Tammy's spectacular gardens were featured in the first garden book, *Simply Country Gardens*.

The living room trim is painted with an Olde Century milk paint called "Sugar House Brown". Tammy found an early picture of this room and when they rebuilt the fireplace, they angled it as it had been originally built. The mantel is one of the beams from the house which is all post and beam construction.

Tammy likes the patina of Olde World Pewter and has many pieces displayed throughout the house. The old gun on the lintel belonged to Tammy's Dad. The tin wall sconce was from Katie's Lighthouse.

Tammy's upholstered furniture, shown above, is from Johnston Benchworks. A large crafted crow sits on the edge of an early trencher made by Primitiques. The coverlet on the table is from Family Heirloom Weavers.

Tammy purchased the hanging barn lantern for the shop and an extra for herself. It is a Ginny Curry piece. The feather tree stays up all year which Tammy justifies because it is filled with bird ornaments.

Tammy divides the living and dining areas of the large room with a pine drop leaf table. The pewter candelabra is a favorite and an Olde World Pewter piece. Tammy and Vic purchased the large oak farm table and chairs at a local Amish store. She reported that the Amish almost choked when she asked them to paint the cherry table base black.

Tammy purchased the fabric animals at Curry's Antiques.

Tammy leaves the twig tree up all year too and even turns the lights on during a gloomy summer day to brighten up the room and her spirit. The tree is filled with birds made by Barbara Stein. A friend made the hooked rug, which says the name of the shop, as a gift. Some of Barbara Stein's fabric fruit is also arranged in the large dough bowl made by Primitiques.

The hutch cupboard belonged to Tammy's grandmother and is filled with new pieces of redware.

A goose, purchased at Ginny Curry's, nests in a large trencher. The black table candleholder is a replica of those used on a stagecoach. It can be totally dismantled for easy storing and then quickly reassembled when needed.

A blackened wax pineapple, made by Marsh Homestead Country Antiques, sits at the edge of an early dresser belonging to Tammy's grandmother. The electric tin candelabra was made by The Tin Peddler of Ohio.

The den is where Tammy and Vic spend most of their time and where comfortable furniture was a must. The trim paint is Olde Century "Barn Red". A blue chest in the corner belonged to Vic's mother who also made the hanging quilt as a gift to Tammy.

The window treatments on the sun porch are from Curry's Antiques. Tammy would like to make this room more primitive but has comprised with Vic who insists on some comfortable wicker. Tammy calls this room "her happy room" and sits here every morning before work to enjoy her expansive gardens and pond in the back of the house. Tammy's aunt made the large braided rug in the center of the room.

The camelback love seat is from Johnston Benchworks. The platform sheep on the side table is from Arnett's Country Store.

Tammy uses woven coverlets from Family Heirloom Weavers on the bed. The watercolor print is called A Smart Turnout and reminds Tammy of her grandfather who raised horses and owned a sleigh.

An early cedar chest at the foot of the bed holds an iron candlestick made by Kathy Nugent of Primitives and a barn lantern from Ginny Curry.

Tammy elects not to use dressers but prefers cupboards to store clothing.

Tammy's bathroom is quite large and allows for Tammy to accessorize with country pieces. The claw foot tub is dated on the bottom to the turn of the century. I noted the hanging light and asked Tammy how she managed to conceal all the electrical wires. I was surprised and very pleased to learn, as I used them in my remodeled home, that Katie's Lighthouse makes iron hooks which are hollow and allow for the wiring to be threaded through the inside. They can be purchased in any length and make a huge difference in the overall appearance of hanging lights.

Tammy's kitchen is at the side of the house and adjoins a small breakfast nook.

Redware with a yellow glaze by Wisconsin Pottery and a Ginny Curry lantern are displayed on the reproduction dry sink which Tammy uses to create a barrier between the entranceway and the working kitchen area. It also provides a back for the island holding her stovetop as can be seen in the picture below. The hanging black tin Whaler's Lantern was made by Katie's Lighthouse.

Tammy's kitchen cabinetry is cherry and was custom-made locally.

Tammy added a mantel and faux fireplace to add a feeling of warmth to the breakfast nook.

Tammy and Vic's home is a perfect example of how a warm country decor can be achieved without the need to find early authentic pieces. Given a choice, Tammy would love to have more antiques in her home but regardless, her skill at decorating with reproductions is an inspiration for anyone who feels that "only new will do".

Chapter 9

Karen and Rich Boulay

Karen and Rich Boulay live in what was the circa 1840 Hillsville School #7 in Spencer, Massachusetts and are the fourth family to live in the transformed home. Karen had always dreamed of living in an older home and operating a shop where people would feel welcomed – a place for family and friends to visit and relax. When the school closed its doors, the town utilized the building as a grange hall and finally sold the school in 1946 for a price of $1,255. The original owners purchased the house and remodeled it into a residence. The house had been vacant for a year and a half when Karen found it. She saw it one night, made an offer and moved in four weeks later. Karen grew up in an Early American style home, decorated by her Mom and Dad, so she was used to being in an atmosphere that was warm and cozy. When she looked for her first home, she knew she wanted that same atmosphere, but in a period home. Karen had spent twelve years making and designing primitive pieces which she sold to the retail trade and country collector. As she searched for the right home, she also had in mind that she wanted to open her own shop within the walls of that home. The Spencer home

seemed like the perfect spot to blend her antiques and her primitives. Ideally it was large enough to house that shop Karen had always dreamed of owning.

Karen began immediately to decorate one room at a time and did most of the work herself. After living in her home for 16 years, Karen is still remodeling and feels this is her passion. She may never be quite finished as she always finds something that can be changed or moved around. A little over a year after moving in, Karen opened her shop at one end of the house, *Primitive Thymes*. When I arrived to photograph the house, Karen was preparing for her Harvest Gathering Open House and the yard was thoroughly dressed with primitives , harvested pumpkins and bittersweet.

A few years after Karen opened her shop, she met Rich and discovered that they shared a common interest in old houses. Karen has been amazed at how quickly Rich picked up on the design and operations of running the shop. Rich particularly enjoys working with the customers and works right alongside of Karen in all the operations of the shop. Rich, although he works full time as a Senior Research Assistant with St. Gobain, manages to find some time to build furniture and some of the country wooden pieces for sale in the shop. He and Karen hope to both retire in another two years and have the time to devote to their business.

When you enter the front door, you step into a large vestibule with the six room shop to the right and the living quarters to the left. In the sitting room, Karen painted the walls with a paint from The Seraph called "Linen" then glazed the walls with the same color as the trim to age them. The trim is a mixture of colors that Karen hand mixed to get the color and depth she was seeking. Karen said she loves experimenting to get different old primitive looks on the walls, ceilings and in the rooms in general.

In each room, Karen glazes the walls with the same color paint she uses on the trim. She feels this gives the room an aged appearance while carrying the color throughout the room. Karen's primary goal in each room is to provide a setting where everyone can relax and feel at home. She seeks to always incorporate nature throughout the house and feels that style most clearly reflects how our ancestors would have adorned their homes. Rich and Karen's home is decorated primarily with reproduction pieces but she has added a few antiques and blended them nicely.

For example, while the large settle in black paint which houses the television is a new piece made by Jack Fisher of The Rusty Roosta *in West Brookfield, Massachusetts, the piece in the opposite side of the room is an early dry sink which came out of a tannery in nearby Leicester, MA. It was dismantled and moved in pieces to the Boulay's home. The surface was not salvageable and Karen was forced to paint the piece.*

Karen has decorated the dry sink with country primitive accessories, many made by Jane Wallace of Old Mother Hubbard, *and mixed Jane's work with other textures with drieds.*

The Keeping Room extends across the back of the house. Karen used Benjamin Moore 'Greenfield Pumpkin" paint on the trim and also for the glazing on the walls. The couch is from The Seraph in Sturbridge, MA. The floor cloth was made by Michelle Hollick of New Hampshire. The drop leaf table, from an old ice cream parlor in Delaware, is treasured for its honey toned patina.

The box is an early wood bin from the Amish and was found in Delaware. Karen has filled it with pumpkins, gourds and drieds.

The chair in the corner is the Vermont chair made by Angel House. An antique drying rack hangs above it and holds dried herbs and tobacco leaves.

Dirk Dishop of Ohio made the shelf which holds redware pottery from nearby Old Sturbridge Village and a garland of dried green string beans called 'leather britches'.

The large settle in the corner is designed with a pull down writing desk on which Karen has placed an inkwell and quill pen. Karen added a tall quilt rack behind to add height. The stoneware crock is an original Norton Co piece and a favorite of Rich's as his current employer was the former Norton Company. The mail pouch, as well as many of the dolls Karen and Rich sell in the shop, was made by Eva Ramsey of Pine Patch Primitives.

This is Rich's favorite corner of the house. The antique cast iron stove was a gift from a friend who once owned a shop in Sturbridge. After Karen was unsuccessful in getting it approved to use as a heat source due to housing codes, she added electric logs and is amazed at how realistic they look. The black creates a wonderful backdrop for the colors of the harvested produce and bittersweet.

Rich made the hanging black cupboard after a request from Karen who stated there was an empty spot on the wall that needed something. Karen and Rich both find this an enjoyable corner to decorate because it lends itself to using naturals and primitive accents.

Peeking in the doorway at one end of the Keeping Room, the laundry room has been decorated with early parts of washers, wooden ironing boards, sock stretchers and other items you might see in a room used for doing the wash.

Karen and Rich's kitchen is filled with handmade primitive accents. Karen is adamant about selling only handmade pieces in their shop similar to those made 200 years ago. She carries that style into their home as well. Old wooden bowls are filled with dried gourds, real pumpkins and bittersweet.

The winnowing board on the stove was made by Primitiques of Pennsylvania. The lighting is from Timeless Lighting. Karen's sink is a composite granite sink made by Franke and sold at Lowes. Rich made all the counters which replaced the harvest gold formica Karen acquired with the house. However Karen has decorated the counters so heavily that Rich occasionally asks her to "please take some things off so we can see my handiwork.

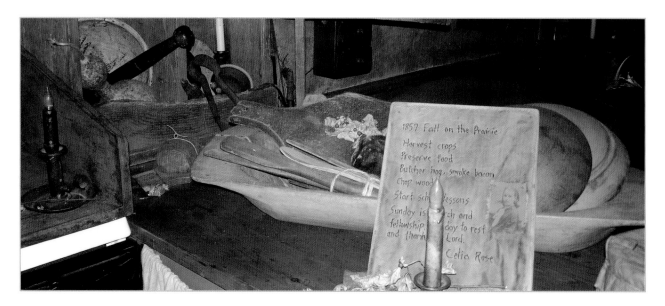

An antique butter worker sits on the island.
Karen uses curtains made of 'prairie homespun'
to cover some of the cabinets and give the
kitchen an earlier look.

Baskets, bowls and drieds from Karen's herb garden hang from an original chestnut beam in the kitchen, adding further to that 'prairie' look in the kitchen and Keeping Room.

The glass front cupboard was made by Andy of Good Intent Farm in Pennsylvania. It houses pottery and kitchen accents.

The hutch in the corner of the dining room was dismantled and came from the same tannery as the dry sink in the parlor. The table top is made with old floor boards from a late 1700's schoolhouse in New Hampshire.

Karen used paint from The Seraph called 'Ochre" in the dining room.

The corner hutch makes an ideal spot for Karen's extensive collection of pewter.

The large wooden trough and old crock make great decorating pieces which Karen changes with the season.

The old wooden bowl has a make-do handle and is one of Karen's favorite pieces because of its unique qualities. The bowl and accessories sit atop an old drying rack.

The hanging mustard cupboard is an old piece and retains its original paint.

The pickle crock was found in Delaware and still has its original wooden top.

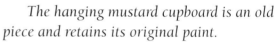

Karen's office on the second floor is her retreat. The antique desk rests on a base made by a local artisan. Karen finds the tranquility of her office soothing when she is forced to do the paperwork associated with running a business.

The master bedroom is a few steps up from the second floor level. The four poster bed was made locally. A tall early six board chest stands at the foot. The long neck goose on the bed was made by Druann McCarty of Cinnamon Creek Cabin.

Karen has created a quiet and visually appealing corner in one area. She has added wool cloaks, textiles and baskets amidst a vintage spinning wheel. The walls are painted with Benjamin Moore "Alexander Beige" with "Hasbrook Brown" on the trim.

The bathroom is painted with Benjamin Moore "Sage Green" paint. Karen has glazed the walls here as well and applied the paint with a sea sponge. She is careful to add heavy coats of paint in the corners and on areas where people might have touched the walls.

The cabinet in the bathroom was a gift from an elderly woman Karen took care of many years ago. While the cabinet is not as early or primitive as Karen would choose, it holds a special sentiment.

The guest room is warm and inviting. Karen wanted to decorate it in a way that would welcome guests and make them feel comfortable.

Homemade dolls are displayed on the bed.

An Angel House chair, shown above right, provides a quiet corner for reading.

Karen and Rich's six room shop is filled with accessories and some furniture. Karen and Rich's shop is ideal if you are seeking handmade pieces and bowl fillers as 90% of what is sold is hand made in the USA. If there is an imported piece, it has to be good enough for Karen to place it in her own home. Karen says her customers have come to expect homemade. Karen and Rich host two Open House events each year. Their Harvest Gathering, which includes a candlelight house tour and refreshments, is always in September. Over the Thanksgiving weekend, Friday-Sunday, the annual Open House, A Very Prairie Christmas, now draws second and third generations. One tradition Karen and Rich have established is that they choose one child that weekend who touches their hearts. They give that child a gift which might be something his/her accompanying adult indicated they would like. Once or twice Karen and Rich have chosen a child who holds a few dollars with which to purchase a gift and when that child selects an item, miraculously it is the exact cost of what the child has in his hand to spend.

Primitive Thymes *is located at 4 Northwest Street in Spencer and is open Thursday-Sunday or by appointment or chance. The hours are Thursday and Friday, 10-3; Saturday, 10-4 and Sunday, noon-4. The phone number is 508-885-4958. Karen and Rich conduct their business with the philosophy that they don't have customers, they have friends. Their welcoming home and shop reflect that sentiment beautifully.*

Glossary

Some readers have asked if I would provide a glossary of terms and definition of pieces that are unfamiliar to them. I've decided to occasionally add a Glossary at the back of a book and am happy to accept suggestions. Many of the names for pieces are derived from the purpose the piece served or something the piece resembled. Many are derivatives of a foreign word. Hopefully these simple descriptions will help clear up confusion.

Chinking

Chinking refers to the process of applying a mixture of clay, lime and sand to fill narrow openings in between logs in a log home. Synthetic chink is now available.

Hutch Table

A hutch table is as it sounds; a combination table and chest. The chest at the bottom used for storage gave the piece its name. The top tilted up and was held upright with large wooden pegs.

Jenny Lind Bed

Jenny Lind furniture is named after Johanna Maria Lind, a Swedish opera singer who lived from 1820-1887. She was so popular throughout the world that manufacturers began to name furniture after her. Today Jenny Lind beds are still being made and characteristically have wood turnings. Sometimes the beds are also called spool beds.

Lindsey Woolsey Fabric

Lindsey Woolsey is a wool fabric which has been woven with linen to make the fabric more durable. The word derives from the words linen and wool.

Mule Chest

A mule chest saved valuable space. It consists of a lift top chest on top and two drawers at the bottom. There is much speculation as to why these chests were named what they were. One theory is that they were used to store 17thC slippers which were called mules. Another is that the chest could hold as much as a mule could carry. A third theory is that a mule, a hybrid of a horse and donkey, typified the hybrid combination of a blanket chest and chest of drawers.

Ogee Mirror

These mirrors were named after the type of molding used to frame them. The moldings consisted of an S shaped profile.

Onion Bottle

Onion bottles in the 17thC and 18thC were free blown which means blown without seams. They are bulbous shaped like an onion. The glass looks to be black but often is dark olive or amber. The glassblower used a rod called a punty on the end of which he would put a glob of glass to hold the bottle while the neck was being formed. When finished, a drop of water added to the glob would break the bottle free creating a pontil, or indent, on the bottom of the bottle. There are many types of pontils. For example, a ground polished pontil would be found on expensive pieces such as vases and decanters while a Rough pontil might not be as finished.

Peel

A peel, or baking paddle, was used for sliding lumps of dough neatly in the oven so that the bread would look good when baked. Peels have been used for thousands of years and were made of wood with long handles for reaching into the deep ovens.

Rat Tail Hinges

Hinges which are named after their resemblance to a rat's tail

Sawbuck Table

The sawbuck table has X shaped legs and is a very primitive piece usually found on a covered porch rather than in the interior of a house. The plank top was often made from used boards. An authentic sawbuck table will most likely have random empty holes in the top where nails had been and the wood will show rust marks from the early nails.

Settle

There were many forms of this piece of furniture but each consisted of a wooden bench with a high back and arms. There was a box with a lift-top under the seat used for storage. Someone would 'settle' on the bench.

Trammel

A trammel is an iron adjustable and saw toothed hook used to hold pots from a fireplace crane. Some have been repurposed and used as a candle holder.

Wedding Band Hogscraper

The hogscraper candlestick was one of the most common in the 17th-19thC. It was named as it resembled the tool used to scrape the hide of a hog in preparation for cooking. Many had a hook at the top making it possible and convenient to hang it over the edge of a chair. The wedding band was the brass piece added around the neck making it more valuable than a piece without the band.

Windsor Chairs

Windsor chairs began to be simplified in the early 19thC and were made as either a side chair or armchairs. The seat was a solid piece of wood. The legs and back are inserted into drilled holes in the seat as opposed to standard chairs where the spindles of the back and the back legs are continuous. It is thought that wheelwrights in the 17th-early 18thC started to make chair spindles in the same fashion as wheel spokes. The first chairs of this type were made in Windsor, Berkshire in the early 18thC and thus the name a Windsor chair. Today the name refers to the style of chair rather than the town where it is thought to have originated. There are numerous styles. A few of the most popular are seen below.

Birdcage Windsor Chair

The birdcage Windsor chair was the design of the rod back with two main uprights in the back. It resembled a birdcage in design.

Bow back Windsor Chair

The bow back Windsor was introduced in the late 18th C in Philadelphia. It has bamboo turned legs and stretcher base. The back was bowed thus giving it its name.

Comb Back Windsor Chair

A perfect example of a piece of furniture named for what it resembles. The back of this style Windsor resembles the shape of a comb used either for the hair or to separate flax.

The "simply country" book series
by Judy Condon

The Place We Call Home

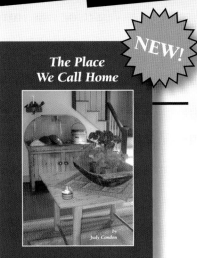

The Place We Call Home features 9 homes. The book demonstrates how each of the homeowners has created a home reflective of their ancestry, interests and what they each hold dear in their heart.

What's in the "simply country" book series?

Country on a Shoestring
33 tips on how to decorate on a shoestring

Of Hearth and Home
mantels, old painted pieces, signs and primitives

A Simpler Time
log homes, bedrooms, kitchens, dining rooms, folk art and stencils

Country Decorating for All Seasons
holiday doors, porches, mantels, trees, vignettes; summer gardens, and fall decorating

As Time Goes By
The Keeping Room; boxes, baskets and bowls; The Privy; Hallways and Small Ways; The Guest Room

Country at Heart
The Tavern Room; early looms, dolls and bears; The Gathering Room; a kitchen aged to perfection; country gardens

Welcome Home
Over 350 photographs from 2 Connecticut homes and 5 Ohio homes.

Home Again
A house tour book featuring 1 Maine home and 7 Ohio homes including a never before photographed Shaker collection.

The Warmth of Home
3 Massachusetts homes, 1 Pennsylvania home, 3 Ohio homes, 1 New York home and 1 Delaware home

The Country Home
6 Ohio homes, 2 Massachusetts homes, and 1 New Hampshire home

The Comfort of Home
Over 325 color photographs showing a Massachusetts and Ohio home of two exceptional collectors. A Maine home; three Massachusetts homes, one of which is in the city.

Simple Greens – Simply Country
Over 400 color photographs of country homes decorated for the holidays. Also a chapter on "how to make a country bed" and the recipe for the large decorative gingerbread boys and pantry cakes.

The Country Life
The home of antique dealer, Marjorie Staufer of Ohio and Colette Donovan of Massachusetts is featured, as well as 4 other Massachusetts homes, a Maine home, a New Hampshire home and a Connecticut home of children's book author, Mark Kimball Moulton.

Simply Country Gardens
Over 500 color photographs of "just country gardens" from twenty-three homes.

The Spirit of Country
A house tour format book featuring homes in Virginia, Maine, Connecticut, Indiana, Ohio, Massachusetts, New Hampshire and Kentucky.

The Joy of Country
Over 400 pictures of homes in Wisconsin, Upstate New York, Ohio, a Connecticut 18thC home, a doublewide in Delaware, 5 Massachusetts homes, a Pennsylvania home and a Maryland home converted from a 19thC granary.

Holidays at a Country Home
The third holiday book in the series consists of over 500 color photographs of 13 decorated homes and a Condon traditional secret recipe!

A Touch of Country
This book features 8 homes. A unique collection of stoneware and weathervanes is included in one home; primitive settings and collections of early paint are highlights. Rug hookers will love one of the chapters and the avid antique collector will marvel over a Maine home!

Back Home – Simply Country
The renovated 19thC New England cape of Judy and Jeff Condon is featured along with eight other country homes.

Just Country Gardens
Just Country Gardens is the second garden book in the series. It features over 550 color photographs from 21 homes and gives background information on each gardner in their chapter.